HOW? WHO? WHAT? WHEN? WHERE? WHY?

Questions kids ask

ABOUT
INVENTIONS

PUBLISHER	Joseph R. DeVarennes	
PUBLICATION DIRECTOR	Kenneth H. Pearson	
ADVISORS	Roger Aubin	
	Robert Furlonger	
EDITORIAL SUPERVISOR	Jocelyn Smyth	
PRODUCTION MANAGER	Ernest Homewood	
PRODUCTION ASSISTANTS	Martine Gingras	Kathy Kishimoto
	Catherine Gordon	Peter Thomlison
CONTRIBUTORS	Alison Dickie	Nancy Prasad
	Bill Ivy	Lois Rock
	Jacqueline Kendel	Merebeth Switzer
	Anne Langdon	Dave Taylor
	Sheila Macdonald	Alison Tharen
	Susan Marshall	Donna Thomson
	Pamela Martin	Pam Young
	Colin McCance	
SENIOR EDITOR	Robin Rivers	
EDITORS	Brian Cross	Ann Martin
	Anne Louise Mahoney	Mayta Tannenbaum
PUBLICATION ADMINISTRATOR	Anna Good	
ART AND DESIGN	Richard Comely	Ronald Migliore
	Robert B. Curry	Penelope Moir
	George Elliott	Marion Stuck
	Marilyn James	Bill Suddick
	Robert Johanssen	Sue Wilkinson

Canadian Cataloguing in Publication Data

Main entry under title:

Questions kids ask about inventions

(Questions kids ask ; 13)
ISBN 0-7172-2552-6

1. Inventions—Miscellanea—Juvenile literature.
2. Science—Miscellanea—Juvenile literature.
3. Children's questions and answers.
I. Smyth, Jocelyn.   II. Comely, Richard.   III. Series.

T48.Q48 1988   j609'.02   C89-093164-X

Questions Kids Ask ... about INVENTIONS

continued

Do you have to do well in school to be an inventor?

Not necessarily. Thomas Edison was a boy who was curious to find out how things worked and asked adults lots of questions. When he was seven and went to school, he drove his teacher crazy with all his questions that he only stayed for three months.

After that, his mother tutored him and he worked hard by himself to find the answers to his questions. He used his knowledge to invent over 1000 things, including the electric light bulb and the first record player, called a phonograph.

But remember: Edison only stopped going to school. He never stopped learning and studying!

DID YOU KNOW . . . the first sound recording was the nursery rhyme "Mary Had a Little Lamb." Edison recorded it when he invented the phonograph.

Who invented potato chips?

In 1853, George Crum was a chef at an elegant hotel in Saratoga Springs, New York. One day, he made some French fries for a customer. To his annoyance, the customer sent them back. "They're too thick," was the complaint. George made the next batch thinner. The customer sent those back, too. "Still too thick."

George was getting cross. "I'll show that customer not to complain," he thought, and made the fries so thin they were very crisp and hard.

To his surprise, the customer was delighted. George Crum had invented potato chips.

Is it possible to invent something by accident?

You might be interested to know the story of a scientist named Alexander Fleming. He was doing experiments with bacteria that cause disease. One day, one of the dishes where he was growing bacteria went moldy. What a failure! He was about to throw it out, when he noticed that the mold had killed the bacteria close to it. From this discovery, he went on to invent a medicine that would kill bacteria and so cure many illnesses. The medicine was penicillin, the first type of antibiotic.

Who invented Band-Aids?

Do you know people who are always getting cuts and scrapes? Earle Dickson's wife seemed to have lots of little accidents in the kitchen and he wanted to be able to help her quickly and easily.

The company he worked for made bandages, but they were huge ones for serious cuts. Earle cut them up and used tape to stick small bandages over minor cuts.

When his company heard of the idea in 1920, it decided to make the sticky bandages for sale. The company was Johnson and Johnson and the new product was Band-Aids.

Are there shoes that you can wear to walk on water?

Imagine wearing a canoe on each foot! About 50 years ago, a man named Harold Strohmeier invented *skijaks*. They are a cross between skis and kayaks. You wear one on each foot, just like skis. However, instead of using ski poles, you paddle through the water. When you are an expert, you can even try shooting the rapids!

Who invented the submarine?

Perhaps you could say that no one person invented the submarine because there were many experimenters in many countries. Human beings seem to have dreamed almost forever of a boat that could travel under the waves, but for centuries no one could solve the obvious problems. How do you make it watertight? If you can make it sink, how do you make it float again? And how do you propel it and steer it underwater?

The first submarines were designed and built in Europe in the 1600s and early 1700s. They were not meant as warships but their potential as a weapon that could attack unseen was soon recognized. As early as the American Revolution in 1776, a man named David Bushnell developed a sort of one-man submarine called the *Turtle*. It was not very effective. Nonetheless, the idea was picked up again over 80 years later during the American Civil War when the Confederate Navy used several crude submarines, also rather unsuccessfully.

Despite these early failures, submarine experiments continued. By 1914, all large navies had efficient submarines, and the First World War showed what terribly powerful weapons they were. The military development of submarines has gone on, but in recent decades people have also built research subs to explore the ocean depths.

When were balloons invented?

Can you imagine floating high up in the air and drifting wherever the wind takes you? Well, that's what it's like to travel in a balloon.

The first large balloon was built in 1783 in France by two brothers, Joseph and Jacques Montgolfier. It was made of paper and cloth. After it was held over a fire it filled with hot, smoky air. Since the hot air in the balloon was lighter than the air around it the balloon rose. The brothers were very pleased. Next they hung a basket beneath the balloon to carry passengers. They placed a rooster, a duck and a sheep inside and filled the balloon with hot air. The balloon floated high above the ground until the air inside it cooled. Then it floated back down and the animal passengers returned to earth. Soon after, people began going up in hot-air balloons.

At the same time Jacques Charles, a French scientist, invented the gas balloon. It was safer than hot-air balloons because it didn't use fire to warm the air. Instead it used a gas that was lighter than air—hydrogen. Charles built his balloon out of rubberized silk and filled it with hydrogen. He tied sand bags to the passenger basket which could be dropped to make the balloon go higher. A valve at the top could be opened to make the balloon go lower.

Ballooning became a very popular sport. People traveled across oceans and performed daring feats in them. Balloons were also used for observation and scientific research.

Modern balloons are made out of rubber, nylon or plastic and filled with hot air or helium. And the balloon still follows the wind.

DID YOU KNOW . . . toy balloons were first made hundreds of years ago in China out of paper.

Who invented chewing gum?

People have been chewing gum for thousands of years. The ancient Greeks chewed a gum made from the sap of the mastic tree. The American Indians of New England taught the settlers to chew a gum taken from the hardened sap of the spruce tree. More than a thousand years ago the Mayan Indians of Mexico chewed chicle, the sap of the sapodilla tree.

In 1860 the Mexican general López de Santa Anna brought chicle to the United States, where he hoped to sell it as a type of rubber. He gave some to Thomas Adams, a druggist in New York. Adams boiled the chicle in an attempt to make it into rubber, but it wouldn't harden. Instead of rubber, they discovered that chicle made an excellent chewing gum!

11

Who invented firecrackers?

Like many inventions, firecrackers were first made by accident. Over 1000 years ago, a cook in China combined three ingredients commonly found in a Chinese kitchen of that time: sulfur, charcoal and saltpeter, or potassium nitrate. Whatever the cook was trying to make went up in smoke and a shower of sparks—it was gunpowder!

Soon the Chinese were filling hollow bamboo stalks with the three chemicals, which exploded in the air and produced a beautiful display of light and sparks. Fireworks were set off to celebrate, and to frighten away evil spirits. By adding other chemicals to the basic recipe, the Chinese produced colored fireworks.

DID YOU KNOW . . . the Chinese did not use gunpowder for military purposes. It was a Franciscan monk in Germany who began using it in this way during the 1200s.

Who invented matches?

Matches have become part of our everyday lives—we use them to light fires, candles, gas stoves and firecrackers. We can't imagine living without them, but less than 200 years ago, there was no such thing!

There are two kinds of matches: safety matches, which only light when scratched against a certain surface, and strike-anywhere, or friction, matches, which work when struck against any rough surface.

An English pharmacist named John Walker made the very first friction match in 1827. It was an 8-centimetre (3-inch) stick of wood with a chemical mixture on one end. It worked, but it caused sparks to fly and it smelled terrible.

Charles Sauria of France improved on this match in the early 1830s—or so he and everyone else thought. His matches burned longer and the phosphorus on the tips didn't smell. Unfortunately, it produced poisonous fumes that caused a deadly disease. Hundreds of factory workers had their health ruined before a nonpoisonous substance was found to replace the phosphorus.

Safety matches were invented in 1855. They were still poisonous, but at least they reduced the number of fires caused by matches being lit accidentally.

DID YOU KNOW . . . mice can light strike-anywhere matches by gnawing on them.

13

Whoever thought of inventing Velcro?

One day in 1948, a Swiss mountaineer named George de Mestral was walking in the country. He looked down at his socks. Bother! Prickly little seed balls called burrs had stuck to the fabric. He had to sit down and pick them off. As he did, some of them stuck to the cuff of his jacket. They would stick again and again.

This gave him an idea. If he could invent a piece of tape that was fuzzy like his socks, and another piece of tape that was prickly like the burrs, they could be used to fasten things together.

It took years of work to get it just right, but the tape he invented—Velcro—was finally perfected and has many uses today.

And you always thought Velcro was invented by someone who couldn't tie shoelaces. Right?

14

Who invented perfume?

No one really knows who invented perfume, though we do know that ancient peoples burned wood and spices for the sweet smells given off by the smoke. The word perfume comes from the Latin words *per fumus* which mean "through smoke." We also know that the Egyptians used perfume over 3000 years ago because it has been found in the tombs of their pharaohs.

Perfumes were first brought to Europe in the 13th century by the Crusaders. The powerful scents quickly became popular because they masked the unpleasant smell of unbathed people and filthy cities. By the 16th century, Europe was making its own perfumes from flowers, fruits, spices and other natural materials. The first artificial perfumes were made in the 1800s. Today some types of perfume are worth more than their weight in gold.

Who invented braille?

Braille is a special alphabet in which each letter is made up of an arrangement of raised dots. Blind people can feel the dots and recognize the letters so that they can read.

It was invented by Louis Braille in 1824. He had been blind since he was three years old. At age 15, he invented this method of communication so that people like him, who could not see, could enjoy reading books.

When was writing invented?

We think that writing was invented independently in at least four separate places, at four different times. The earliest writing was invented in ancient Egypt, where people wrote sentences made of complicated pictures at least 6000 years ago. Later, they developed a system of simpler forms of these pictures, writing with a brush and ink on a sheet of pounded plant fiber.

Writing was also invented very early—at least 5000 yeas ago—by a people called Sumerians in the land that is now the country of Iraq. They developed a complicated script of lines and dots, probably because of the materials they used. They wrote with a metal point on wet clay tablets, and if you ever tried that, you'd know how hard it is to make anything *other* than lines or dots.

Somewhat later, but again independently, writing was developed in China, where people wrote complex pictures with ink on paper. This writing is still in use, but today no one can even understand the writing of the fourth group of people who developed this idea. These were the Mayans of Central America, and like much of their civilization, their writing is a mystery to us.

Who invented Christmas cards?

Sending and receiving Christmas cards every year is now a custom, but it wasn't always so. People used to exchange holiday greetings in person; later they sent handwritten notes through the mail. In 1823 the head of the United States Post Office complained that because of the increased volume of mail at Christmastime, he would have to hire 16 more mailmen to deliver them.

The first printed Christmas card was designed in London, England in 1843. Printed cards quickly became popular in England, then in Germany, but it wasn't until 1875 that printed Christmas cards gained popularity in North America. That year, Louis Prang, "the father of the American Christmas card," began printing and selling cards with colored pictures on them. Since then, billions and billions of Christmas cards have been sent the world around.

Who invented the bicycle?

The first bicycle was invented in about 1790 by a Frenchman, the Comte de Sivrac. It was called a *célérifère,* or a wooden horse. It had no pedals: riders had to kick their feet on the ground to make it go. Adding to the thrill was the fact that there was no way to steer it and no brakes!

Since then, many inventors have added improvements to create the type of bicycle you ride today: brakes, handlebars, pedals that are linked to the wheel, gears, rubber tires, a padded saddle, and much more.

DID YOU KNOW . . . the fastest bicycles can travel at about 100 kilometres (60 miles) an hour. The bike is very low and the rider lies backwards inside a lightweight shell that looks like a little racing car.

Who invented the wheel?

The wheel was invented so long ago that we have no way of knowing who thought of it first. There's no doubt about one thing, however—the wheel is one of the most important inventions ever. Just think of the difference between carrying a heavy load of groceries and being able to pull it home in a cart.

Our earliest ancestors carried anything they had to move—and so they probably didn't move very much. At some point, they got the idea of using animals like donkeys, horses and oxen to move heavy loads. Then, about 6000 years ago, it happened: somebody made a cart, something an ox could pull, and then put wheels under it, so that the same ox could pull a much heavier load. Around the same time, someone first made pottery on a potter's wheel. It's possible that the invention of the potter's wheel came first.

The first wheels were solid, but after a while people figured out how to make spoked wheels which were much lighter. This happened around 5000 years ago, probably somewhere in the area of the modern countries of Iraq, Iran and Pakistan.

How did the Frisbee get its name?

When Walter Frederick Morrison invented a toy disk that would fly through the air, he called it a Flyin' Saucer. It was designed to look like a spaceship from another planet.

He was in for a surprise. When the company that sold Flyin' Saucers for him visited Yale University in Connecticut, the salesperson found students already playing a flying saucer game. They used old pie tins made by the local Frisbie Pie Company and yelled "Frisbie" every time they made a throw.

Soon the new plastic Flyin' Saucer was renamed "Frisbee."

Who invented portable cassette players with earphones?

The people at the Japanese firm of Sony were disappointed. They had been trying to make a miniature version of their cassette recorders. The part that played cassettes could be made small, but the part that recorded could not. They decided to forget the idea.

One day, an important person in the company heard about their research. He had a clever idea: sell the miniature cassette players with earphones so people could listen to their favorite music as they walked around.

What a success! No one even thought to ask why the new "Sony Walkman" didn't record anything.

When was the toothbrush invented?

For thousands of years people have been taking care of their teeth by brushing them. The first toothbrushes were twigs that were frayed at the end to make "bristles." They were called chew sticks.

Not until 500 years ago did people try making toothbrushes with bristles. There was a problem: pig's bristles were too hard and horse hairs were too soft. What would make a really good bristle?

The first toothbrush with nylon bristles was invented in the days when your grandparents were young: in 1938. Over the years, toothbrush makers worked hard to perfect the nylon bristles so they felt just right and did a good job.

DID YOU KNOW . . . chew sticks are still used in some parts of the world, including Africa and remote parts of the United States.

Has anyone invented a really good way to get people out of bed?

Imagine a cold, stone building with no heating. Imagine that it is wintertime and you have to get out of bed very, very early in the morning to go and say prayers.

About 1000 years ago, monks in Europe had to deal with this problem. They had water clocks that measured the time by the amount of water that fell and they linked these up to a gong. Clang, clang, clang: the first alarm clock was invented.

Much later, people invented mechanical clocks that could chime, play a little tune, or let out a noisy ring. Today, you can get electronic clocks that buzz, beep, or even turn on your radio. A few will make you a hot drink.

You still don't want to get out of bed? Maybe you need a bed that lifts up at the pillow end and tips you feet first onto the floor!

BONJOUR
GOOD MORNING

Who invented frozen food?

Frozen food wasn't strictly invented: it was discovered!

Between 1912 and 1916, a man named Clarence Birdseye traveled throughout Labrador. He noticed that the Indians of the region caught fish that would freeze in the sub-zero temperatures. As long as it remained frozen, the fish remained good enough to cook and eat.

After years of experimenting he perfected a method for quick-freezing food. In 1925, Birdseye started selling small, compact boxes of frozen fish.

DID YOU KNOW . . . a man named Frank Epperson invented the popsicle in 1905. He left a glass of lemonade with a mixing stick in it on a windowsill one cold night and in the morning, there it was: the first popsicle!

Who invented the snowmobile?

Joseph-Armand Bombardier suffered a tragedy. His young son died because he could not be taken to hospital during a snowstorm in Quebec. Bombardier was determined that the same thing should not happen to anyone else. It took him a lot of work to get the design right, but finally, in 1930, he made a machine that would do the job. It looked like a motorbike on skis and used traction to travel through the snow.

The snowmobile has become a very useful form of transport for people who live in snowy regions. It is used to deliver mail, for emergency services and also for the sheer fun of speeding over the snow.

Who invented blue jeans?

At one time, blue jeans were mostly worn by cowboys, farmers and miners. Today almost everyone owns at least one pair of blue jeans.

The man who invented them was Levi Strauss, who came to the United States from Bavaria in 1847 when he was 17.

Strauss saw the need miners had for a sturdy pair of canvas pants. He hired a tailor to make a pair, and soon he was in business. Everyone seemed to want a pair of Levi's pants, so he opened a factory to mass-produce them.

Always looking for ways to improve his product, he found a strong but soft and comfortable cloth in a small town in France called Nîmes, pronounced "neem." It was called *serge de Nîmes* (cloth of Nîmes), shortened to "denim." Strauss switched to using denim in his factory. He dyed it blue and started a new fashion and a new industry!

The name "blue denims" was changed to "blue jeans" when Levi switched to a similar cloth that came from a town in Italy called Genoa, which French weavers called Gênes. This is the origin of our word "jeans."

Who invented zippers?

A century ago, people used buttons and laces to fasten their clothes, shoes and boots. Boots had buttons from top to bottom, so putting them on and taking them off took a lot of time.

The first zipper, patented in Chicago in 1893 by an engineer named Whitcomb L. Judson, was designed to replace buttons on boots. It was called a "slide fastener" and was made of metal. Nobody paid any attention to Judson's invention.

Twenty years later, Swedish-American engineer Gideon Sundback designed a lighter, more dependable fastener. There were still problems with it, though. Made of metal, the fasteners rusted easily. To avoid this, people unstitched them from their garments before washing, and sewed them back in when the clothes were dry. Also, because they were such a new idea, manufacturers had to attach instructions to any item that had one.

Rustproofing solved the first problem in the early 1920s, about the same time as the B.F. Goodrich Company began to make galoshes with slide fasteners. Because of the "zipping" sound the slide made when it was pulled up and down, the company called them "Zipper Boots." The name caught on, the fasteners became zippers—and who today could imagine life without them?

27

Who invented Raggedy Ann?

Marcella Gruelle was 13 years old and she was sick. Her father decided to write a story to cheer her up. It was about a little girl who had a doll called Raggedy Ann. When Marcella's Aunt Prudence heard about it, she made the first Raggedy Ann doll as a present for Marcella. The Raggedy Ann type of doll has been a best friend to thousands of children for over 70 years.

What is the difference between a discovery and an invention?

Making a discovery means that you find out about something that already exists. (Even if a few people already know about it, you will be considered the discoverer if you are the first person to make it widely known.) Coming up with an invention means that you make something that is entirely new.

For example, the ancient peoples of Central America discovered cacao trees growing in the area where they lived. They also discovered (perhaps by accident) that they could make a flavored drink by soaking the seeds of this tree in water. About 400 years ago, European explorers discovered Central America, its people, the cacao trees and the drink, cocoa.

DID YOU KNOW . . . M&M's were named after their inventors, Forrest *M*ars and Bruce *M*urries. M&M's were invented in 1940.

About 150 years ago, people in Europe thought about new ways to use the cacao seeds, or cocoa beans. They found a way to grind them up and mix the paste with milk and sugar to create—you guessed it—solid chocolate. Since then, people have been inventing all kinds of wonderful candies from chocolate.

DID YOU KNOW . . . Thomas Edison's first major invention was a stock ticker for printing stock-exchange quotations in brokers' offices. He was 21 at the time and he received $40 000 for his patents.

Where do inventors buy the parts they need for their inventions?

You've hit on a real problem! Because inventors are making something that is entirely new, they usually have to make the parts themselves using whatever they have.

Less than 50 years ago an Englishman named Christopher Cockerell had the idea that he could build a machine that would travel on a cushion of air. For his first successful experiment he used a cat food can, a coffee can, a vacuum cleaner and kitchen scales.

From this strange beginning, he went on to design the air-cushion vehicle, or Hovercraft.

Do inventors become rich and famous?

Not always. Even if you invent something really wonderful, you will have to work hard to become rich and famous. You will have to make lots of copies of your invention and sell them. You will also have to make sure that no one else copies your great idea. Still, there is hope. In recent years, a young man named Bill Gates invented such wonderful new ways to program computers that he became the world's youngest billionaire just a few years after he left school. That means he had more than $1 000 000 000! Think what you could buy with that!

Index _____